OUR AMISH

Values

Who we are and what we believe

Lester Beachy
LESTER BEACHY

1st Printing	June 2013	4M
2nd Printing	February 2014	8M

ISBN: 978-0-615-80221-3

For additional copies visit your local bookstore or contact:

Lester Beachy
3468 Township Road 166
Sugarcreek, OH 44681
330.852.4148

Photography: ©Doyle Yoder Photography *unless otherwise noted*

Design and Layout: Rosetta Mullet

Printed by:

Carlisle Printing
OF WALNUT CREEK LTD
800.927.4196 · carlisleprinting.com
Sugarcreek, Ohio 44681

PREFACE

Our community gets over four million visitors a year. At the Amish and Mennonite Heritage Center near Berlin, Ohio, we meet people from all over the world and from all walks of life, many of them wanting to learn more about the Amish people. Some come knowing very little, while others have read books or watched films about the Amish people and may be misinformed by popular fiction or entertainment.

I was pleased to hear that a member of the local Amish community had written a book addressing the questions we so often hear from visitors. Not only will this give readers an accurate and sincere account of how we live and why we live the way we do, but it corrects some of the more common misconceptions.

The Amish are a very diverse people. *Our Amish Values* captures the flavor of Holmes County, Ohio, the largest Amish community in the world and also one of the more diverse communities. Visitors planning to visit our community will benefit from this book. It will help them to better understand the community they are visiting.

To God be the glory!

–Mark Oliver—Amish and Mennonite Heritage Center

INTRODUCTION

It has now been several years since I first agreed to be a tour guide at a local tourist site. It is something I have enjoyed very much. There are a tremendous number of tourists that come to our Amish country. What brings them here?

Some come merely out of curiosity, somewhat like taking a trip to the zoo. Others have a high respect for us and appreciate the many values that we teach and hold on to. Then there are those who can appreciate our spiritual emphasis and the way we strive to serve God and to live separate from the world.

Many locals can put up with all the traffic because of how tourism boosts the local economy. Some local merchants exploit the Amish name to sell their products.

When I lead a tour, one of the first things I try to tell them is that I welcome their questions. This gives me a better idea of what they wish to know. Usually they have many questions. Unfortunately, there is a lot of incorrect information in some books that have been written about us. That is one reason for this book. I have covered a broad field and hope I have done justice in representing the Amish.

The reader must keep in mind that there are many different groups of Amish in many different states and that practices will vary a lot from one group to the next.

I enjoy meeting people from all over the world. My tour guiding has enabled me to meet many interesting people. I especially enjoy international groups. I look at this as an opportunity to be a witness for Jesus Christ. Many tourists want to know why we choose to live this way. I can freely share our beliefs and values with them.

—Lester Beachy

CONTENTS

ANABAPTIST

We Amish trace our heritage to the Reformation period. While Martin Luther was bringing reforms to the church in Germany, his counterpart, Ulrich Zwingli, was also bringing changes to the church in Switzerland.

Despite the changes brought about by these men, there was a group of concerned brethren who felt the reforms were falling short of completely following the Scriptures. Eventually, this group started their own church and called themselves the Swiss Brethren. Later, because of their emphasis on adult believers' baptism instead of infant baptism, they became known as Anabaptists *(rebaptizers).*

The Anabaptist movement was an earnest endeavor to get back to the Scriptures. In addition to adult believers' baptism, they believed in separation between church and state. They also refused to take up the sword to defend themselves.

Many were severely persecuted and hundreds gave their lives for the truth. This persecution was carried out by both the Catholic and Protestant churches. Despite the persecution, the movement took root and spread.

Martin Luther's German translation of the Bible and the invention of the printing press contributed much to the growth and spread of the Anabaptist movement. Thanks to these, the Scriptures became available and affordable for even the common people.

BUGGY

The Amish use horse and buggy for transportation. Unlike my grandfather, who bought his first buggy from Sears, we now have skilled Amish craftsmen who build our buggies.

A new single-seat buggy can cost up to $4,000, but it will last a lifetime if taken good care of. The buggies will vary some in style from one group of Amish to the next.

There is a 12-volt storage battery to provide lights, and most buggies are equipped with hydraulic brakes to help when going downhill.

We do not believe the automobile is wrong in itself—it is the fast-paced lifestyle that we wish to avoid. By refraining from ownership of the car, we endeavor to live a more slow-paced life.

If we need to travel a greater distance than our horses can take us, we hire a taxi to take us. There are non-Amish people in our community who make their living from doing taxi work for the Amish.

Most of the horses that we use for our buggies are standardbred horses. They are either not fast enough for the racetrack or are retired from the track. Most horses can be used until they are 18 to 20 years old. There are dealers that buy them from the racetracks and then resell them to the Amish.

CHURCH

In our Holmes County Amish community we do not have church houses. Instead, we have church services at our homes and take turns hosting the service. Today many Amish have a shop building to have the services in.

The average church will be from 25 to 40 families, with well over a hundred people. Services start at 9 AM and last until around noon. There is no nursery; even small children learn to sit quietly.

Each church district has four ordained men—a bishop, two ministers, and a deacon. These four all help with teaching the Word and leading the church. They are ordained from among the congregation by using the lot and letting God do the choosing. It is a lifetime position and is unsalaried.

We have a bench wagon that is used to transport benches from one place to the next. Whoever hosts the church services provides lunch. Eating a meal together and visiting is a vital part of the Amish church tradition.

In our services the men sit on one side and the women on the other, facing each other. There is preaching, prayer, Scripture reading, and singing, using songs written by our Anabaptist forefathers. Services are normally conducted in our *Pennsylvania Deitsh* dialect.

DATING

There is a period of dating before marriage. Dating standards or practices vary a lot from one order of Amish to the next.

In our New Order Amish circle the youth do not date before becoming a church member, and also not before they are 18 years old. There is no social dating. The boys lead out in finding a life companion; a girl would never ask a boy for a date. There is no physical contact before marriage.

A typical date would be the boy coming to the girl's home for the Sunday evening meal. After supper they would go to the Sunday evening hymn singing for the youth. After the singing they would come back to the girl's home for a snack and visiting. Before the boy leaves for home, they read from the Scriptures and have prayer together.

It is common to date anywhere from one to two years before marriage. After engagement, wedding plans are made, with the wedding at the bride's home. There is an earnest seeking of God's will before dating and marriage.

Not all Amish will marry. For some, God has chosen the single life. Whether we are single or married, the important thing is to seek God first. Therein we find fulfillment in life.

EVOLUTION

Since the Amish believe the Bible is God's Word, and that it is infallible, we do not believe in evolution. We believe that each individual is divinely planned and created, and that God has a plan for each one of us.

We believe evolution comes from the evil one—Satan—and that those who believe and teach it have been led astray. In simple faith we believe the truth of the Bible, that we are created in the image of God.

Death is not the end, but rather a step into the very presence of God. That which we see darkly here will then become reality. How should we then live? The answer is found in the Bible, God's Holy Word. Romans 12:1 sums it up well: *I beseech you therefore, brethren, by the mercies of God, that ye present your bodies a living sacrifice, holy, acceptable unto God, which is your reasonable service.*

It is a tradition among the Amish that at every communion service, marriage service, and funeral service we are taught how God created everything by His spoken Word.

To us it is simply a matter of faith, of taking God at His Word. If we discard this solid foundational truth, we have no foundation upon which to stand. How anyone could really believe that everything just happened by chance and that man evolved over millions of years is totally beyond our comprehension. Taking God at His Word gives direction and hope to one's life.

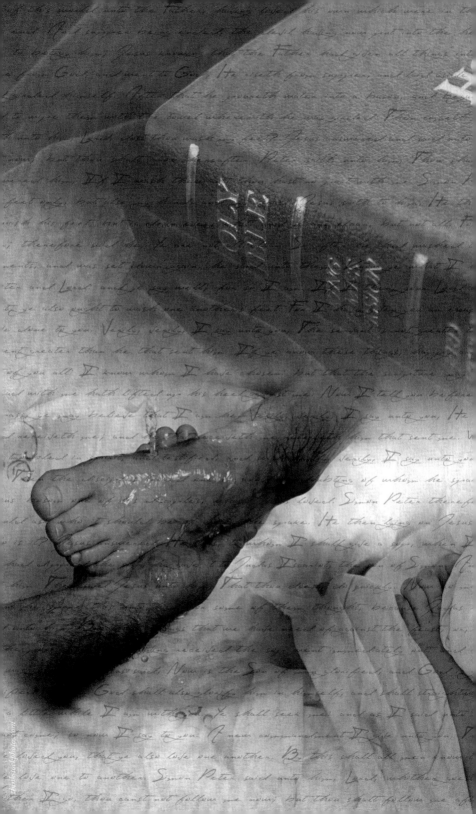

FOOTWASHING

In John 13 we read of an unusual occasion which the disciples, especially Peter, had a hard time understanding. They had just finished supper when Jesus arose, girded a towel around Himself, and with a basin of water proceeded to wash the feet of His disciples.

Later in this chapter Jesus told His disciples that He had done this as an example and that "ye should do as I have done." Having Jesus, their Lord and Master, wash their feet was a lesson in humility and servanthood.

Twice a year in our communion services, we commemorate the suffering and death of Jesus by partaking of the sacred emblems of bread and wine. And then at the end of this special day we wash each other's feet.

Brother with brother and sister with sister, we take a basin of water and a towel and stoop down to wash each other's feet. We are all on one level, young and old, rich and poor, feeble and strong. We are all on the same plane; no one is better than the other.

It is a practice that our Anabaptist forefathers preserved and handed down to us. It is a direct command from Jesus Himself, and we feel blessed to observe and obey.

GMost Amish grow a lot of their own vegetables. Not only is it healthy, but there is also a great satisfaction and accomplishment in raising your own food.

The main vegetables are corn, peas, beans, potatoes, and tomatoes. Many people also have a strawberry patch. A garden plot is an ideal place for families to work and share together.

We all know that you can't just stick some seeds in the ground, then forget about it and several months later reap a bountiful harvest. That's not exactly how it works. Ever since the fall of man we have had weeds to contend with. It involves some sweat and toil.

It is important to prepare the soil by adding manure or compost. We can also be sure that weeds will come. We don't have to plant those. Just as sinful desires automatically take root and grow in everyone's life, so it is with weeds.

Don't ever let weeds take over, and certainly don't let them go to seed in your garden. If they do you have more work cut out for the next year.

What a great satisfaction it is in the late summer or early fall to enjoy the harvest. Remember, it is God who created seeds after their kind and makes them increase. We only provide the labor. Shelves filled with jars of food for the long winter are a blessing from God.

H
HOLIDAYS

The question of whether we observe holidays and how we observe them is frequently asked by tourists. Yes, we certainly do observe holidays.

Christmas is a day to celebrate the birth of our Redeemer. Although it is doubtful that Jesus was born on December 25th, we do believe it is very proper to set aside a special day. We do, however, try to stay away from the commercialization of the Christmas season.

Although, some gifts might be exchanged, Santa Claus has no place among us. Neither do we have a Christmas tree or other so-called Christmas decorations. Family gatherings are often held on Christmas. It is a day of rest from physical labor.

Easter is also a special day of celebrating the resurrection of Jesus Christ from the dead. All Amish churches have communion services at Easter time. It is the goal of the Amish to keep holidays Christ-centered and focused on the true meaning of the day.

Ascension Day and Good Friday are also special days. In contrast to the modern trend, we observe Sunday as a day of rest. How special and refreshing it is to rest from physical labor on the first day of the week and to focus on worshiping God. He alone is worthy of our worship.

**I**MMIGRATION The Amish came to America because of the wonderful opportunities that were offered them, especially religious freedom. Persecution in Europe had scattered them and made life very difficult. As early as 1683, some Anabaptists came to America on a ship called the *Concord*.

But coming to America was no easy decision. It was difficult for whole families to come, and individuals that set sail probably did not expect to see their loved ones again. Plus, the journey by boat was extremely perilous. The first Amish settled in eastern Pennsylvania. Many later traveled on west to Somerset County, Pennsylvania, and from there to Ohio and beyond. Later, immigrants came directly to Ohio and other states farther west.

The first Amish man to move to Holmes County, Ohio, was Jonas Stutzman, who settled just south of Walnut Creek, Ohio, in 1809.

Today there are Amish in at least 30 states, plus some in Canada. Crowded conditions in some of the older settlements are causing some Amish to look for opportunities elsewhere. Starting new communities can be an outreach and a great opportunity to be a witness in a new area.

One reason new settlements burst forth is to provide the possibilities to farm. In our older communities, land prices are very high, making it difficult for anyone to make a living on the farm.

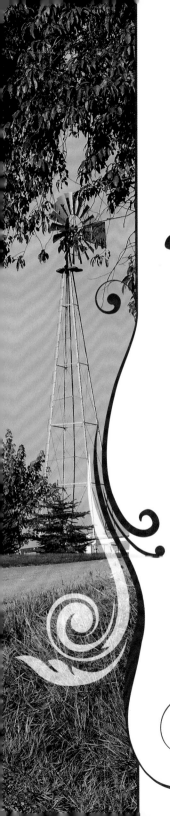

JEWELRY

Amish women wear no jewelry at all. The reason for this is purely based on the Word of God. Both the apostles, Peter and Paul, address this subject. In I Timothy 2:9 Paul writes that women should not adorn themselves with gold or pearls or costly array. In I Peter we read that the women's adorning should not be the outward adorning of wearing of gold.

Paul writes that women should be modest and sober. Peter writes that women should have a meek and quiet spirit, which is in the sight of God of great price (I Peter 3:4).

I remember several years ago some of us traveled to New York City to sing and witness for Christ. One young lady from the city remarked how pure and beautiful the Amish ladies looked. A plain, modest dress with no jewelry or makeup is a witness for Christ without even using words.

A common question is how do we know if a person is married or not if we don't wear wedding rings. True, we may not know at first, but we don't have to. In our church services the married and those not married sit separately. Plus, we have some separate activities for the youth.

KEEPING

Are we Amish going to be able to keep and maintain our way of life and values? With modern technology pressing in on us from all sides and threatening our plain lifestyle, will we be able to resist, and if so, how?

We Amish do make changes. One example would be when we allowed mechanical milkers for the dairy farmers. We realize we do need to be able to make a living. The challenge is to not let technology control us. Not being hooked up to the power grid is a help in this.

Ultimately it is the responsibility of the church to make and maintain standards to live by and guide us. These standards, known as the *ordnung* of the church, vary considerably from one Amish church group to another.

When we do make a major change in church *ordnung*, we will vote over it. For the change to be made, we need 100% unanimity. We believe there is a lot of strength in a unified decision.

When thinking of our children and the following generations to come, if the Lord tarries, it is well worth the effort it takes to keep our plain lifestyle. We do not base our salvation on our way of life. Instead, we choose this lifestyle because we are God's children. We trust it will be possible to keep our plain way until Christ comes.

LANGUAGE

Our mother tongue is a German dialect called *Pennsylvania Deitsh*. It is not Dutch as so many have written and said. We as a whole are not Dutch people. In the southern part of Germany there is a present-day dialect very similar to what we speak.

We speak our mother tongue at home and in everyday life. English is usually learned either in school or from older siblings.

The singing and Scripture reading in our church services are in High German, while the preaching is in *Pennsylvania Deitsh*. If we have visitors who do not understand our language, we usually have part of the services in English. This happens from time to time.

We don't add any new words to our language, so we are using more English words today than we did 20 years ago. One example would be the word *computer*. We just use the English word.

Our language has in recent years become a written language. A former Amish man with linguistic training developed an alphabet and has translated the Scriptures into our dialect. This major project is just now in the finishing stages.

We believe that keeping our language is central to maintaining our separate culture and lifestyle.

MARRIAGE

Marriage is a lifetime commitment. We vow to love and care for each other as long as we both shall live. Divorce is not an option.

However, we are just as human as anyone else and there are problems in some marriages from time to time. The Bible has the answers for us if we adhere to it. We do have a counseling place run by Amish ordained men for couples that need help.

If a marriage partner passes away, the other partner is free to remarry.

Amish weddings are usually held at the home of the bride and are quite large, with up to 600 guests invited. In our New Order Amish circle, weddings are often on Saturday. Other Amish groups are more likely to have the wedding on a weekday. Weddings are usually in the spring or fall.

There are numerous wedding trailers or kitchens on wheels that can be rented when you have a wedding. These trailers have tables, stoves, cookware, and other supplies that are needed. Also, many have a cooler on one end and a small freezer.

The wedding meal is a special meal usually consisting of chicken, mashed potatoes, and dressing, plus desserts. Church ladies and neighbor ladies are assigned to help prepare the meal.

The young couple will usually rent a place until they can buy their own property.

NONRESISTANCE

Being non-resistant means that we resist not evil. This is what Jesus taught in the Sermon on the Mount in Matthew 5:39. Peter writes that we render not evil for evil (I Peter 3:9). We are told to turn the other cheek to return good for evil. In accordance with this, we refrain from bearing arms.

We are conscientious objectors to war. We feel we are called to save lives, not to take lives. This was a deciding factor for many Amish who came to America. To them, religious freedom sounded almost too good to be true.

We are extremely grateful to God and our government for the freedom we have to live as we believe the Bible teaches us.

We pay our taxes and try to obey the laws of our land, but if our government asks us to kill, we decline in an honorable way. There was a time when our young men were drafted and some of them suffered severe trials because of their refusal to bear arms. During later times our young men were able to serve for two years in hospitals.

We believe that Jesus both taught and modeled nonresistance. We humbly strive to follow His example. He always, in every circumstance, responded in love. As His children, may we strive to do the same.

O

There was a time when up to 95% of the Amish lived on farms. In our large community today it is more like 5%.

When my grandfather was a young married man back in the 1920s, you could milk a few cows by hand, raise some pigs, have a few extra laying hens, and make a living. It's a little more complicated today.

I realize people lived a lot simpler then, and life was slower paced. Things like medical care and dental care have skyrocketed in price. We Amish could also do with a lot less today if we chose to do so. Our lifestyle has also changed, albeit not as fast as society around us, and we need larger incomes to make a living. It's not so easy to make a living on the family farm, although those who have good management do well.

Many Amish do carpenter work or other types of construction, and Amish-made furniture is prized far and wide.

We have a strong work ethic and try to teach our children to work with their hands. Working together as families is very valuable to us. Unfortunately, factory hours have changed our lifestyle and there is a lot more free time in the evenings. On the plus side, there is also more time for traveling and going on family trips.

PLAIN We are known as the plain people. This often refers to our dress, but it also applies to other areas of Amish life. Simplicity is another word that conveys a similar meaning.

We believe that God's children should and will be separate from the world (Romans 12:2, I Peter 1:14, and I John 2:15-17). The world lives for self and exalts selfish goals and desires. God's children desire to crucify self and bring honor and glory to God, who alone is worthy.

That is why we dress in a plain, modest attire. We seek to avoid bright, flashy, attention-seeking colors. Our goal is to cover the body so as not to draw attention to the person. Our plain dress often gives opportunities to speak for God to others.

Just a century ago there was not as great a difference in the Amish dress and society around us. But many changes have come through the influence of television and other means, and general society has drifted away from godly convictions and biblical truth.

In our farming practices we have smaller family-oriented operations. Farming with horses puts an automatic limit on the size of our farms. Most Amish farms and homes are neat and well kept.

Inside, our houses are plain and clean. There are pictures on the walls, often with a Scripture verse.

QUIVER

By using quiver here I am referring to the Scripture verses in Psalm 127:4-5. "As arrows are in the hand of a mighty man; so are children of the youth. Happy is the man that has his quiver full of them: they shall not be ashamed, but they shall speak with the enemies in the gate."

Amish as a whole have larger families than non-Amish. Children are welcomed and loved in our Amish communities. Not only are they the church of tomorrow, but they are a vital part of the church today. Churches with no children or youth will not exist for long.

The Amish population is doubling about every 22 years, largely due to our larger families. I am often asked what the average family size is. The answer, I would guess, is about six children.

Women have three options for delivery; a midwife coming out to the home, a local hospital, or there are also several birthing centers in our area.

Father, Mother, and children working, eating, and worshiping together can be a little heaven on earth. But children are born with a sinful, selfish nature that needs to be broken. Children need training and discipline. Again we find that the Scriptures have the answers. Spanking in love will often bring the desired results. Undisciplined children often don't contribute positively to society later in life.

RUMSPRINGA

RWhen talking to tourists this word comes up repeatedly. Seemingly many non-Amish are under the impression that at a certain age, I assume around 16, it is the expected and accepted practice of Amish youth to have a period of several years to experience what's out there in the world.

They may get a radio or even a car and go to movies and what not. They often even wear non-Amish clothes.

I have never read any Amish romance novels, so I don't know exactly what picture is portrayed in most of them. But I get the picture that *rumspringa* is way overblown. It makes a story that sells.

Although there are Amish communities where this is the accepted practice, in our Amish circle it is not expected, and youth who take that route are not obeying their parents. I'm not saying it never happens, but it is not the accepted norm.

Are we depriving our young people by denying them this freedom? I don't think so. It's much better for them not to sow wild oats than someday reaping a bitter harvest.

We provide Bible studies and hymn singings and occasional social activities for our youth. As a whole they also join church at a younger age than they did 50 years ago. All in all, there is a lot less *rumspringa* than there used to be.

SCHOOL There are at least three options for Amish children to receive their schooling. Most Amish children go to our own private parochial schools. Some choose to send their children to a local public school and still others take the home school route.

We have our own Amish teachers. Most of them are single girls who will teach a few years before they get married. Each school has a board, usually three men who are responsible to hire teachers and to keep the school running smoothly.

Amish children only go through eighth grade. We really don't need more formal education for the type of jobs we have. It's not that we are against more education, we just go at it a little differently after eighth grade. It's more of a hands-on experience, working with the parent or learning a skill.

The average school has about 30 to 40 pupils, with a lower grade teacher and an upper grade teacher. The teachers are allowed to and expected to discipline. This includes spanking if the offense warrants it.

The schools are supported by the parents and churches. The teachers are paid a modest salary. Regardless of how we do our schooling, we all have to pay public school tax even if we don't use the public school.

We don't emphasize sports as the public schools do. Our children are there to learn. Most of the subjects taught in our schools are similar to those taught in public schools, such as math, reading, English, and social studies. There are differences, however; you will never find a class where evolution is taught—but you might find pupils studying a horse and buggy safety driving course.

TRADITION Webster defines tradition as the handing down of knowledge, beliefs, and customs from one generation to another. We Amish have many traditions. Some traditions that crept in among us such as bed courtship were definitely not good. Thankfully, such traditions can be changed.

We do have many good traditions and customs that if discarded would eventually cause us to lose our identity. There have been Amish who wanted to get away from all tradition. But just as they threw tradition to the wind, so that same wind blew them to points hither and yon.

Some traditions that pertain to how we conduct our church services would be the slow tunes that we sing in unison. There is some mystery as to where these slow tunes originated. Also, the song leader starts every line and then the rest of the congregation joins in.

The way we dress is largely tradition and custom. We believe it conforms to the scriptural teaching of modesty and separation. But we do not believe it is the only way that is right.

The tradition of helping each other when there is a tragedy is certainly one we wish to maintain. We are widely known for our barn raisings when fire destroys a barn or other structure.

When there is a death in a family or community we all pitch in. Meals are provided, chores are done, and funeral preparations are made. The list could go on and on.

UNIFORMITY How do we maintain uniformity in dress and practice? Maybe we first need to ask why it is necessary to keep unity. We do have a Scripture in Philippians 3:16: "Nevertheless, whereto we have already attained, let us walk by the same rule, let us mind the same thing."

For a group to remain separated from the world and its influences, and to be separated unto God, there must be a unified effort. Left to individual choice and preference there will be disunity and eventually scattering to the four winds.

So how do the Amish maintain unity? By laying down individuality and self-will. It means the surrendering of myself to the group consensus. For the spiritual well-being of my soul and the souls of my family, we develop a group consensus. Therein we find protection and shelter.

In order to keep this unity, the erring ones must be disciplined and brought back into line. This is the responsibility of the ministry, with the help of the whole body.

There might be some differences from one congregation to the next, but there is an effort to maintain community uniformity.

In our church we have a written set of standards or rules that we maintain. Twice a year, in the spring and in the fall, we are reminded of what is expected of us. Only if we are unified will we partake of communion.

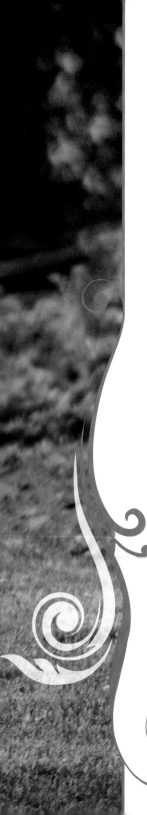

**V**ALUES

To value something is to esteem or regard it highly. We value highly the Word of God. We believe the Word of God holds the key to the inner need of all mankind. It is our road map to heaven. It will never fail. It is just as relevant today as in the day it was written.

We believe it should be read every day, and we are encouraged to memorize portions of it to better resist the wiles of the devil. Families should read it together. And of course the Bible is read and taught each Sunday.

Families and children are valued highly. We can't take our possessions along to heaven, but we aim to take our children along. That is one of the main reasons we don't have television in our homes. There is too great a potential for harm—too much trash and immorality. If we value our children, we will try to protect them from harm.

We value our freedom in this country. Maybe especially so because of persecution in the past. While we generally don't vote, we believe in separation between church and state. We pray for the leaders of our land. May God grant that they make the right moral decisions for our country.

We value honesty. We simply trust each other. We try to speak the truth. We value integrity and moral purity. We value community, and strive to help each other in time of need. We value our heritage and pray that we can instill these same values in our children.

WOMEN

Amish women as a rule are keepers at home. I remember, quite a few years ago, when my wife and I were at Wooster College answering questions about the Amish. One girl asked my wife, "Don't you ever have a desire to get a career and make something of your life?" That is certainly the prevailing thought in our society. But really, is any career for women more valuable than being a keeper at home?

Before God, both male and female have the same value. It is simply that we have different roles to fulfill. The Bible teaches us that the head of the woman is the man, and the head of the man is Christ (I Corinthians 11:3). In Genesis 3:16 we read that the woman is to be subject to her husband. Colossians 3:18 states: "Wives, submit yourselves unto your own husbands, as it is fit in the Lord."

I believe the greatest responsibility lies on us men. If we love our wife with a sacrificial love, she will find it easier to let us lead, and thus to fulfill her own role. As we fulfill our God-given role, we find that it works. God's plan is always best.

Women do vote in our churches if issues come up, but they do not teach in the congregation. You will not find any Amish women preachers.

The head covering or veiling that every Amish woman wears is a sign of submission to her husband and to God. In I Corinthians 11 Paul writes that women are to have their heads covered.

It would seem ideal if discipline were not needed in the church of God. But even God's children can fall into sin. No one is immune. Satan tempts us in those areas where we are weakest.

In the Amish church, if a member falls into sin and refuses to repent, he or she may eventually be excommunicated. This subject often comes up when people ask us about our way of life. There might be several reasons for this.

One reason is that shunning seems to be greatly overblown in some books that have been written by non-Amish. Another reason is that many churches don't discipline those who err.

We believe that the church needs to be kept pure. The apostle Paul explains this in I Corinthians 5. Notice especially the last few verses in this chapter.

To those not familiar with this type of discipline in the church, there are several aspects I'd like to explain. If a situation arises where shunning is required, it needs to be done in love. It is not an attempt to turn the erring ones away, but to help them come to repentance. They can come back at any time if they repent.

They are not totally avoided. It is in business dealings and in eating with them that a separation is made. It is to remind them of their need to repent and their standing before God and the church. There is great rejoicing when they amend their ways and come back to God.

Youth are a vital part of the Amish church. I have many fond memories of my own years with the youth before I was married. There is a huge hole in our church services when the youth are missing.

Youth are full of energy. How beautiful if that energy can be channeled in a way to serve God and our fellowman. It can be a great help for youth and adults to interact and build good relationships.

We believe that well-behaved youth and good singing go hand in hand. We do not use any musical instruments with our singing, but do teach the basic rudiments of music. Singing can be an effectual way to share the message of Christ. Our youth sometimes go to prisons throughout Ohio and sing for the inmates.

There are also hymn singings on Sunday night for the youth. In the wintertime there is ice-skating. In the summer there will be an occasional volleyball or softball game.

Most youth will get a job at around 17 or 18 years of age. The paycheck comes home to the parents until they are 21 years old. Then they are of age and get to keep their own money. Usually they live at home until they get married.

Most youth in our circle get baptized and join the church between the ages of 16 and 18. We feel by then they are old enough to understand the step they are taking. We believe it is the responsibility of the church to provide the right atmosphere and activities for our young people.

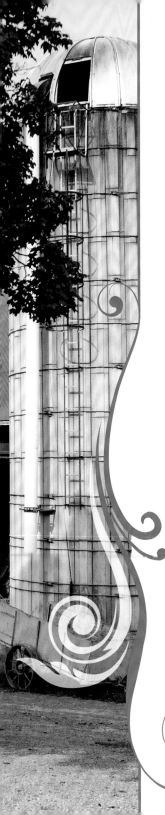

ZEAL

Webster defines zeal as enthusiasm, fervor, earnestness, or a display of great interest. I doubt that any group of people can maintain their way of life without being excited about what they have. We need a solid conviction that our way of life is biblical and has value.

We need to maintain an earnest seeking for a personal relationship with God. Our culture and traditions are empty without a vital relationship with God. We need parents and ministers who earnestly contend for the faith. God desires and has provided everything we need to have that vital connection with Him.

We need to have an earnest zeal in teaching our children to seek God early in life and to have a personal relationship with Jesus Christ. Family is so important in our culture. We enjoy sitting down to a well-prepared meal and sharing our everyday experiences. We believe communicating, singing, and working together as a family are essential for God's blessing on our homes and churches.

It is important that we have a zeal for our church. God wants us to gather together as a body of believers to worship Him. We need to sing together, pray together, and study His Word together. Our ministers need to be enthusiastic and inspired as they lead the church.

If we wish to maintain a zeal for God throughout our life, we need to spend time in His Word every day. His Word is living water for our soul. The deeper we dig, the more our thirst will be satisfied.

Baptismal Vows

1. Can you confess with the eunuch, "I believe that Jesus Christ is the Son of God"?
Answer: Yes, I believe that Jesus Christ is the Son of God.

2. Do you also confess this to be a Christian doctrine, church, and brotherhood to which you are about to submit?
Answer: Yes.

3. Do you now renounce the world, the devil and all his doings, as well as your own flesh and blood, and desire to serve only Jesus Christ, who died on the cross for you?
Answer: Yes.

4. Do you also promise, in the presence of God and His church, with the Lord's help to support these doctrines and regulations, to earnestly fill your place in the church, to help counsel and labor, and not to depart from the same, come what may, life or death?
Answer? Yes.

Marriage Vows

Both are asked this first question:

Can you both confess and believe that God has ordained marriage to be a union between one man and one wife, and do you also have the confidence that you are approaching marriage in accordance with the way you have been taught?

Answer: Yes, from the Bridegroom

Answer: Yes, from the Bride

The Bridegroom is asked:

Do you also have the confidence, Brother, that the Lord has provided this, our Sister, as a marriage partner for you?

Answer: Yes

The Bride is asked:

Do you also have the confidence, Sister, that the Lord has provided this, our Brother, as a marriage partner for you?

Answer: Yes

The Bridegroom is asked:

Do you also promise your wife that if she should in bodily weakness, sickness, or any similar circumstances need your help, that you will care for her as is fitting for a Christian husband?

Answer: Yes

The Bride is asked:

Do you promise your husband the same thing, that if he should in bodily weakness, sickness, or any similar circumstances need your help, that you will care for him as is fitting for a Christian wife?

Answer: Yes

Both are then asked:

Do you both promise together that you will with love, forbearance, and patience live with each other, and not part from each other until God will separate you in death?

Answer: Yes, from the Bridegroom

Answer: Yes, from the Bride

A NOTE FROM THE AUTHOR

I was brought up in the Amish church and as a youth joined the church by making the baptismal vows and being baptized.

My wife Ruby and I have five daughters. At the time of this writing the two oldest are married and live nearby. We have two grandchildren.

I have several hobbies, including reading and traveling. A highlight for me has been traveling to several third-world countries. There are a lot of places I hope to still be able to see sometime.

Meeting people from all over is a highlight. I have had the opportunity to talk to many groups of people about our beliefs and lifestyle. It has been enjoyable and a great opportunity. All glory to God.

The author can be contacted by writing to:

Lester Beachy
3468 Township Road 166
Sugarcreek, OH 44681